W9-DBF-624

Bugs, Bugs, Bugs!

Beetles

by Margaret Hall

Consulting Editor: Gail Saunders-Smith, PhD

Consultant: Laura Jesse, Extension Associate
Department of Entomology
Iowa State University
Ames, Iowa

Capstone
press

Mankato, Minnesota

Pebble Plus is published by Capstone Press,
151 Good Counsel Drive, P.O. Box 669, Mankato, Minnesota 56002.
www.capstonepress.com

1 2 3 4 5 6 10 09 08 07 06 05

Library of Congress Cataloging-in-Publication Data
Hall, Margaret, 1947–
  Beetles / by Margaret Hall.
    p. cm. —(Pebble plus: bugs, bugs, bugs!)
  Includes bibliographical references and index.
  ISBN 0-7368-4251-9 (hardcover)
  1. Beetles—Juvenile literature. I. Title. II. Series.
QL576.2.H34 2006
595.76—dc22   2004029485

Summary: Simple text and photographs describe the physical characteristics of beetles.

Editorial Credits
Heather Adamson, editor; Linda Clavel, set designer; Ted Williams, designer; Jo Miller, photo researcher;
  Scott Thoms, photo editor

Photo Credits
Bruce Coleman Inc./Kim Taylor, 15
Corbis/Michael & Patricia Fogden, front cover; Frank Lane Picture Agency/B. Borrell Casals, 21
Corel, 1, back cover
David Liebman Nature Photography/Roger Rageot, 9
James E. Gerholdt, 5
Minden Pictures/Mitsuhiko Imamori, 19
Pete Carmichael, 11
Peter Arnold Inc./T. Da Cunha, 13
Root Resources/Dennis Mauning, 7
Visuals Unlimited/Bill Beatty, 17

Note to Parents and Teachers

The Bugs, Bugs, Bugs! set supports national science standards related to the diversity of life and heredity. This book describes and illustrates beetles. The images support early readers in understanding the text. The repetition of words and phrases helps early readers learn new words. This book also introduces early readers to subject-specific vocabulary words, which are defined in the Glossary section. Early readers may need assistance to read some words and to use the Table of Contents, Glossary, Read More, Internet Sites, and Index sections of the book.

Table of Contents

What Are Beetles?

Beetles are insects
with hard bodies.

How Beetles Look

Many beetles are brown
or black.
Some beetles are
yellow, red, or green.

Some beetles are as big
as an adult's hand.
Other beetles are almost
too small to see.

9

Beetles have two antennas.
Beetles smell and feel
with their antennas.

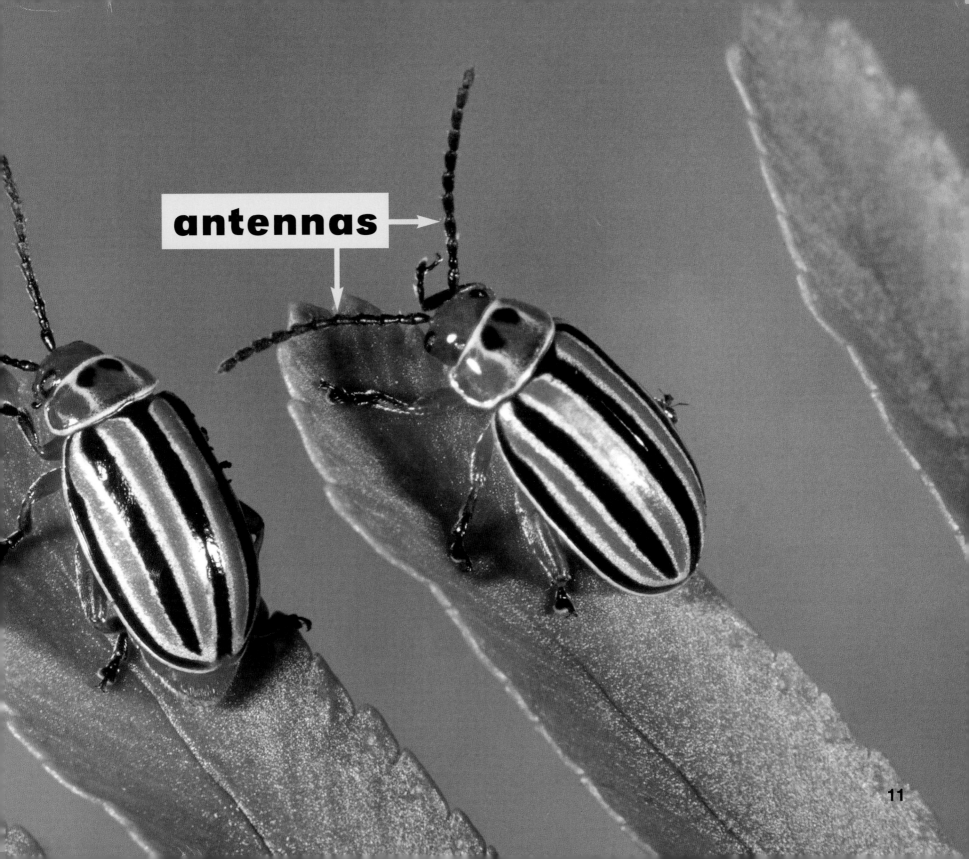

antennas

Beetles have four wings.

Their two top wings

are hard.

top wings

Beetles have two
soft bottom wings.
Beetles use these wings
to fly.

What Beetles Do

Many beetles eat plants or
other insects.
Some beetles even eat
dead animals.

Some beetles have horns.

Beetles use their horns

to fight.

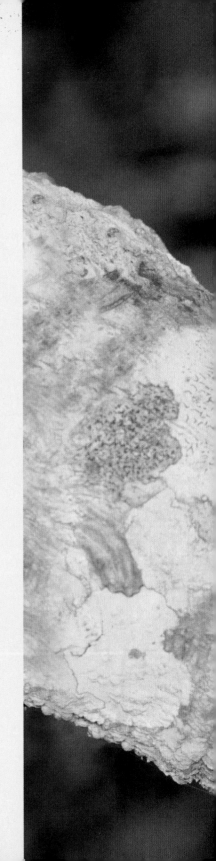

horns

Some beetles

can swim underwater.

Other beetles can jump.

The world has many beetles.

Glossary

antenna—a feeler; insects use antennas to sense movement, to smell, and to listen to each other.

horn—a hard body part sticking out from an animal's head

insect—a small animal with a hard outer shell, six legs, three body sections, and two antennas

wing—a movable part of an insect or a bird that helps it fly

Read More

Derzipilski, Kathleen. *Beetles.* Animals, Animals. New York: Benchmark Books, 2005.

Hipp, Andrew. *Dung Beetles.* The Really Wild Life of Insects. New York: Powerkids Press, 2003.

Prischmann, Deirdre A. *Beetles.* World of Insects. Mankato, Minn.: Capstone Press, 2005.

Internet Sites

FactHound offers a safe, fun way to find Internet sites related to this book. All of the sites on FactHound have been researched by our staff.

Here's how:

1. Visit *www.facthound.com*

2. Type in this special code **0736842519** for age-appropriate sites. Or enter a search word related to this book for a more general search.

3. Click on the **Fetch It** button.

FactHound will fetch the best sites for you!

Index

Word Count: 106
Grade: 1
Early-Intervention Level: 14

HQ